ALL ABOUT

ALL ABOUT RIDING

LEARN TO RIDE—AND RIDE *WELL*

Based on the Yorkshire Television Series by
Dorothy Johnson

With an introduction by
David Broome

STANLEY PAUL/LONDON

STANLEY PAUL & CO LTD
178–202 Great Portland Street, London, W1

AN IMPRINT OF THE   HUTCHINSON GROUP

London   Melbourne   Sydney
Auckland   Bombay   Toronto
Johannesburg   New York

First published 1969

*This book has been set in Imprint type face. It has been
printed in Great Britain at Taylor Garnett Evans &
Co. Ltd by offset lithography at Watford, Hertfordshire*

09 8750 0

Contents

INTRODUCTION BY DAVID BROOME   7

·PRELIMINARIES   9

STAGE ONE Getting the feel of a horse under you   14

STAGE TWO Controlling the horse yourself   23

STAGE THREE Ready for the 'open road'   30

STAGE FOUR Jumping   37

STAGE FIVE Consolidation on the flat   43

STAGE SIX Riding out: keeping control   53

STAGE SEVEN Working the horse   62

STAGE EIGHT Straightening the horse   70

STAGE NINE What next?   72

APPENDIX ONE Stable management window   75

APPENDIX TWO Training the young horse   90

Introduction by David Broome

I have been riding since I was two and a half years old and I long ago stopped thinking consciously about how it is I control and stay on a horse; my body reacts automatically to each situation. This sort of thing applies, of course, to most of the things we do—an experienced car driver, for example, does not *think* about how to change gear; he just does it. It was very different when that same driver was learning.

It is the same with riding. In the early stages of learning you have to concentrate on the *technique* of controlling the horse but as your control improves so does this control become more automatic. Another way of putting it is to say that your hands and legs do your thinking for you. In my own case, for example, I now only think with my head, as opposed to my hands and legs (which then become the instruments with which I *apply* my thoughts) when something is not quite right in the response of the horse during training or practising. Then I may well consider ('ponder', you could say) what I should do, how I should control the horse at a particular point.

But when I watched Mrs. Johnson taking riding lessons during the making of the television programmes, I suddenly realised how different it must feel to the beginner. I noticed a good riding-school horse being ridden by an .advanced learner; the horse was alert and responsive, as he should be, but he was still essentially a quiet, amenable animal—not like some horses I have ridden; the rider was not a complete novice but her 'aids' were not consistent or particularly strong. The horse had spent the last two days in the stables or being ridden on hard surfaces; what difficulty the rider had in controlling him when his hoofs first dug into the moist, soft grass of the field! How he enjoyed the prospect of a good canter! What fun he thought it all was!

I was reminded of how big an animal the horse is, of the power in his back and legs; I compared his physical strength with that of the slight girl who was trying to stay on his back. How strange it must be for the complete novice when she sits for the first time high on the powerful back of this great animal; how wobbly it must feel; how she must wonder about her ability to control him; how frustrating it must be for her to apply the approved aids to the best of her ability and still find the horse unresponsive. 'What is it I must *do* to make the horse understand?' must be her thought.

I realised, in short, just how 'cheeky' human beings are when they attempt to control a horse. I also realised how terribly difficult it must be to learn if the novice is not given good, encouraging instruction. The basics of riding are simple and few; it is their application that presents difficulties.

If you want to ride therefore, and you can take it from me that no one who has learnt regrets it, make sure you are properly taught. Neither this, nor any other book can teach you to ride—only riding can do that. But this book will tell you what being a good rider involves. And, since good riding comes initially through good teaching, it will tell you what to look for in the school you go to.

Sound horsemanship in all its aspects is the basis of the book. Mrs. Johnson does not go into needless raptures about what fine animals horses are nor does she take fruitless pains to describe all those little details which any school will tell you or which you yourself will find out. But if you want to know how best to learn to ride and what you must aim for, you will find her book very useful.

Preliminaries

Riding is clearly and obviously a very enjoyable occupation. There can be few non-riders who would not acknowledge, when asked, that the person is to be envied who can ride and who has access to a horse or pony and even moderately open country. There need be no mystique about this; no romance or sentimentality about 'four-footed friends'. Any fool can see that it is quite simply very good fun when you can do it.

Neither need there be any mystery about learning to ride. It is essentially a simple skill, acquired by a not excessive amount of practice, provided the tuition is sound and the pupil uses his common sense. The pupil who thinks about what he is doing and why he is told such and such will learn far more quickly than he who just follows the instruction unthinkingly.

Neither would it seem difficult to find somewhere to learn this simple and exhilarating skill: riding schools or 'centres', as they are now called, are springing up all over the shop, offering lessons at about 17s. 6d. per hour (N.B. As with everything, look carefully if the goods are offered at cut rate). The average pupil takes about 24 lessons to acquire that state of proficiency which will enable him to do all the basics and give him the confidence which allows him to improve and polish his technique and understanding. Lessons, therefore, will cost in the region of £21, as a minimum.

Every school and instructor has a different method of teaching but the difference between one method and another should not be great. It would tax our ingenuity in the extreme if you and I had to teach someone to boil an egg, using different techniques. This is because the operation is so simple that there is little variation in what one can do and therefore little variation in how it should be taught. Of course, riding is far more complicated than boiling an egg but it is still essentially straightforward—as I said before, there is no mystery attached to it. Therefore your lessons should conform in some fair degree to the course here outlined.

If they do not so conform, then you should ask yourself whether your lessons are providing good value for money. Are you wasting time in that particular school? As in every business there are those who don't scruple over the service they give customers. No diplomas or other qualification are required to teach at a riding school; anyone who has the money to buy horses, and a stable area, can advertise 'Riding Lessons'. This puts you at a disadvantage for, short of personal recommendation, you are often forced to trust to intuition in your choice. You can let this book aid your intuition: use it as a sort of yardstick as to whether the school in general and your instructor in particular are good. It is also worth buying a list of approved schools from the National Equestrian Centre, Stoneleigh, Warwickshire.

General atmosphere is most important, of course. A good school will be a friendly place, aiming to make you feel at home; the teachers will be sympathetic and full of encouragement. Ignore and forget the descriptions given by your father or husband, who remember a hurried and uncomfortable 'crash' course during their army days and talk of the awe-inspiring, rough-riding sergeant major who taught them. Do not put up with a sarcastic instructor, of whom there are too many, for you will not make good progress. Ask for a change and if this is not possible join another school.

What to wear

Riding can be a strenuous pastime and it is important to wear the proper clothes: they will add greatly to your comfort and your progress. It is also important, however, to buy clothes that suit you personally and, therefore, for the first few lessons I think it is better to wear the clothes you already have, borrowing the necessary items you lack. After you have ridden a few times and discussed the pros and cons with practising riders, you will have much more idea of the things you will need. I find that assistants in shops selling riding wear are not expert at advising the novice.

First lessons The most important item is a hard hat. Nowadays most riders prefer a jockey cap because they think it more flattering than a bowler. All good schools will automatically insist that their pupils wear protective head gear, and will keep a supply, so that new pupils may borrow one. If the school of your choice does not make this stipulation then I would suspect it may fall below standard in other respects too. In all events, wear a hard hat—borrow one from a friend if necessary.

A shirt with collar and tie suits most people; if a girl no longer has her school blouses and cannot borrow one from a suitably sized brother, then a roll-neck pullover is most suitable.

Jeans or corded slacks are best because they are less slippery than nylon or other man-made fibres. The drawback to all trousers or slacks is the fact that creases and folds occur when you bend the knee; these form lumps against the saddle and may rub your leg. (This is why you will want to buy jodhpurs at an early stage.)

Footwear is as important as headgear. You need your strongest pair of continuous-soled (through from toe to heel), laced, low-heeled brogues—no studs in the soles. Sandals or slipper-type shoes may slip right through the stirrup iron or fall off the foot, and high-heels (or studs) may wedge in the iron. All these are dangerous and you should not be allowed to ride in them—better borrow a suitable pair.

If you are riding out of doors as opposed to an indoor school, you may need extra clothing. Anoraks are the obvious choice though these are not popular with instructors because they make the pupil look permanently round shouldered. Avoid men's sports jackets—they do not hang properly and you will find you keep sitting on the tail and nearly choking yourself. Avoid ladies' suit jackets—they are too short and make your behind appear too large.

Wear gloves—cotton, string or leather, as plain as possible. They protect your fingers and it is a good habit to start right at the beginning, even if the weather is warm. If your horse starts to sweat (and, of course, if it rains) the reins will become wet and they will slip through ungloved fingers.

Clothes to buy

Hard hat   black is the most serviceable because you can wear it with a black jacket for special occasions in the future. Ladies may prefer navy; brown is very informal. Make sure the hat has the 'Kite' mark inside; this shows that it has been tested for strength and will not become soft after the first fall of rain.

Sports shirt and tie

Jodhpurs   the stretch type are the most comfortable to wear and the easiest to fit (£6 15s.). They can be popped into the washing machine and allowed to drip dry, when they look as good as new. Cotton, or a mixture and cavalry twill are hard wearing and not expensive and, with the latter, you can have a buckskin-type leather strapping inside the knee which helps the rider to sit close to the saddle. Ready made they cost 8 gns. The stretch type are probably the best buy.

Boots   long boots, known as riding boots, are not necessary but, nevertheless, rubber riding boots can nowadays be bought for £5; there is no doubt that they will make you feel firmer in the saddle and may well help improve your riding position. To clean they require only a wipe over in water. I can get quite a shine on mine by rubbing them over with liquid Guard Shine black polish (only a two minute job, whereas leather takes a good 20 minutes polishing). Leather riding boots look much nicer, of course, as they can be made to fit, but they cost up to £50 (though note that ready-made leather boots can be found at 10 gns. if you are a stock size). Jodhpur boots are short ankle boots and again are not necessary; they are comfortable to ride in and cost 5 gns. Their drawback is that they soon wear out if you do much walking in them.

Jacket   this is the most expensive item of normal wear. They vary in style and cut. Do not be persuaded to buy a black or navy jacket—these are for formal occasions—for tweed is far nicer and you will get a better quality tweed for the same money as the navy. Make sure the jacket is long enough: a good test is to hang your arms down by your sides—the edge of the jacket should be low enough just to allow your finger ends to curl round it. When trying it on, sit on a chair arm and put your arms in a riding position, making sure of adequate room across the shoulders. The cost will be between £8 and £15.

Riding mac   This will obviously be desirable in the long run as it is specially designed for riding. But the cost is high and you must decide whether you really want one at this early stage.

Stage One
Getting the feel of a horse under you

The riding-school horse

It is sometimes said that such horses are heavy and dull, because they are used and spoiled by novice after novice. In a good school this is not the case; the horse must and can remain sensitive for all learning purposes. Quiet the horse should be, for obvious reasons, but if you get a 'heavy' horse, ask to change him. If this is not possible, change the school.

Type of lesson

The form of opening, novice lesson you are given will vary according to the facilities available and the type of teaching your instructor prefers. There are three acceptable methods:

On the lunge   This is an individual lesson where you have the instructor all to yourself; half an hour will be long enough. The horse has been trained to work on a large circle at the end of a lunge rein; he moves round the instructor, who has complete control. You will learn very quickly how to sit and follow the movement of the horse, because you can concentrate on this entirely, not worrying about guiding or regulating. You will also gain confidence quickly and feel very safe, because the teacher has full control. Only a minority of schools, however, are able to produce the trained staff and horse necessary for this method of teaching.

Riding in a class I think you will more than likely find you are part of a class; you may be the only beginner but this will not matter because you can watch the others and copy them. A dismounted assistant, walking beside the horse, should lead and help you. If you have never been on a horse before it would be unfair to you and the horse to expect you to cope without a leader.

Riding out on a leading rein This is the old fashioned way, used by the old-time groom who taught the children of the family to ride. Nowadays it may be practised on occasions when the weather has flooded the paddocks or otherwise made them unrideable. You will be mounted on a very quiet horse and your instructor will ride also, leading you on a short rein beside him. He is right beside you and can show you how to sit, etc., but it is impossible to pay attention to detail and it can be uncomfortable if your leg is intermittently squashed in between the two horses.

Mounting

Regardless of the form of the lesson, you ought to be taught the basic fundamentals which will give you the feel of the horse. I hope they will be taught you without too much fuss and over-attention to detail.

First, you must mount. Remember that this can be jolly uncomfortable for the horse! Try to avoid your weight dragging the saddle towards you; take your weight over on to your right arm, well placed on the saddle, and lower yourself slowly and lightly on the horse's back. Remember when you played leap frog, how you staggered when someone landed with a flop on your back!

Do make use of the mounting block—it is nothing to be ashamed of. Much less effort for you and much more comfortable for the horse as it will not pull the saddle across his

15

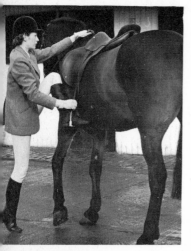

Mounting. Hold the reins in the left hand, throwing them over the horse's neck; point the toe downwards in the stirrup; spring up strongly so that your weight is taken on the right arm. *Below right:* A leg-up. The rider lifts her left calf which is then gripped at knee and ankle; she jumps with the right leg and the spring is helped by the assistant; in one movement she is in the saddle.

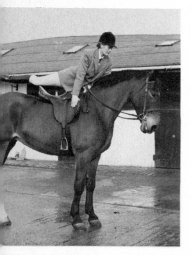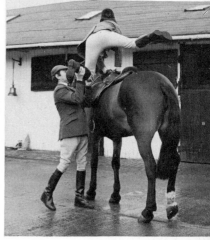

back. It is surprising how many horses are now trained to stand up to the bumper of a land rover, so that their owners can mount.

Position in the saddle

Be patient and try not to become tense if your instructor makes a meal of this. (I suspect, however, that he will be wasting his breath since you will be anxious to get on with the ride and in no mood to concentrate on detail.) Detail is not really called for, either, for if the saddle is of a good pattern you will have difficulty in sitting anywhere but in the centre, which is the correct place—it's as simple as that.

The old-fashioned image of the horseman was of a short, bow-legged and round-shouldered character—and yet all the famous horsemen were tall, long legged and very elegant. Try to copy these—be elegant, grow tall without being stiff. The most difficult part for the beginner is the position of the legs; make sure you understand how to roll the inside of the thigh against the saddle (girls must pull the thigh muscle to the back, so that the flat of the thigh lies close to the saddle flap). Then you will feel wonderfully secure and close to the horse. But, while paying due regard to the position of the thigh, do remember that your seat is to sit on; make sure that it is carrying your body weight and that you *are* sitting on it. The stirrups carry the weight of your legs only.

Length of stirrup

When you are settled in the seat comfortably, then adjust the stirrup leathers so that *they* are comfortable (your teacher will do this for you probably). The right length of stirrup leather is most important—too short and you will sit too far back in the saddle and get behind the movement; too long and you will be loose in the saddle, find it difficult to keep your heel down and tend to tip forward on to your fork.

The correct mounted position: note that shoulder and heel are in line, the stirrup leather is vertical, the elbow and hand are relaxed.

Maintaining position on the move

You will get on much better if you are taught on the lunge for the first lessons because in this way a novice rider develops a feel of rhythm from the word go. Because the horse is kept moving rhythmically and freely, it is much easier for the rider to follow the movement and maintain position. This free rhythm is impossible to produce when the horse is led by an assistant or when taking the horse on a leading rein. Because the instructor has complete control, it is not necessary for you to hold the reins. You will, in fact, feel more secure if you leave them in a loop on the horse's neck and slip your fingers under the front of the saddle.

The aim is to sit still. Keep your balance as the horse moves forward. Think of standing in a crowded bus; as it moves off you tend to fall backwards. Avoid this. Sit heavy on your seat

Common position faults; they are slightly exaggerated
for demonstration purposes.
Above left: Stirrup leathers too short, forcing the rider
to sit too far back.
Below left: Stirrup leathers too short—rider tense and
sitting on fork; note that the horse looks tense too.
Above right: Legs too far forward.
Below right: Stirrup leathers too long, causing rider to
reach for them; insufficient weight upon seat.

Toes turned out, gripping with the back of the leg.
Right hip collapsed; not sitting square.

and then stretch down into your heels; think of moving forward; allow your hip joint to remain soft to allow you to feel the rhythm of the walk. Similarly, when halting (think of the bus stopping suddenly), avoid tipping forward on the horse by again sitting deeply in the saddle and stretching down through the knees, into the heels. Think of the simple fact that your body has been moving forward at about 5 m.p.h., carried by the horse. When stopping, try to stop your body; the trained horse will feel this and will respond. This is called 'bracing the back' or 'using the back'.

Some teachers make a strong point of forcing the heel down but this is not sound advice: the action locks the ankle joint and then all its ability to act as a buffer is lost. Forcing the heel down also tends to make the rider push the lower leg too far forward; this also causes stiffness.

Avoid falling backwards when starting and tipping forward when stopping.

The horse has a stronger body but a weaker mind than you have. Although he responds to your *physical* movements, remember that your physical aids are influenced by your thoughts; therefore the horse is influenced indirectly by your thoughts as well. Think now of leaping with all your might from the seat in which you are sitting. What happens? Your legs, bottom and back tense with your will to do this. Your will, your *belief* in the movement you wish the horse to make, will transmit themselves to the horse through the traditional aids he has learned. These aids are not arbitrary: man has developed them over the years because they do reflect his instinctive reactions. He has had to face the problem of *how* to transmit his wishes to the horse; he has aligned the signals he gives with his own natural reactions.

The thoughts you have are important. Ask obedience of the horse. If you dither mentally, your aids will be muddled and the horse will dither physically.

Trotting

Having coped with the 'walk on' and 'halt' you will not find the actual transition into the trot any more difficult. Although the springy feel of the trotting movement may be disconcerting at first, it will quickly develop your ability to sit relaxed.

Rising to the trot   The French call this 'trot Anglais', the lazy Englishman's way of trotting. But not only is it easier for the rider; it is also easier for the horse. You will have felt a rhythmic trot beat and felt yourself sitting heavy each time the horse's legs strike the ground—1—2—1—2. You will now be taught how to take the weight on to your knee, thigh and down into your heel at every other stride, so that you will rise on 1 and sit on 2. You should be able to master this on the first lesson. But remember that you must anchor the leg below the knee by pushing down into the heel and keeping a bend on the knee. This prevents the leg from swinging forward when sitting and backward when rising, and this swing is what makes a rider flop down in the saddle, which is obviously wrong.

Just as your car is fitted with shock absorbers, so must you develop these in your body when riding. The main ones are in the joints of the hip, knee and ankle, and these must remain soft and relaxed in order that you remain in soft contact with the saddle throughout the trot.

Do not grip inwards. It is wrong teaching technique to encourage the rider to grip the saddle with knee and thigh. As you sit reading now, tense your muscles for grip. What happens? You feel all your seat muscles tighten and force you up out of the chair—or out of the saddle. Never think of gripping; you will do so instinctively when necessary. I repeat—never *think* of gripping.

When rising to the trot, you are doing it wrong if it requires any effort. As you take your shoulders forward on commencement, the movement of the horse will throw you up; the relaxed hip and knee will enable you to return gently to the saddle.

Do not continue to ride when the muscles are tired; you will start to use the wrong muscles and will start to grip, which you mustn't do.

Stage Two
Controlling the horse yourself

During the second lesson you will generally learn the vocabulary of movements of legs and reins which conveys your
wishes to the horse; the signals enable you to control him.
They are called 'controlling aids' and the apt pupil should be
capable of learning the simpler aids and of coming off the
lunge during the last ten minutes of the lesson.

But do not be discouraged if you do not reach this stage, for
it has been my experience that the slow starter often overtakes
the rest of the class. Riders need to develop an awareness of
what might happen, need to have a good imagination, a feel for
the horse, courage and determination; beginners with these
qualities often appear apprehensive and slow.

One thing *is* certain, however: you will not make good
progress during this lesson if you have forgotten or are unsure
of what you practised during the first (perhaps a week ago
and a long time). There ought to be a short period of consolidation at the beginning of the lesson when you must make sure
you are sitting well and have the rhythm of the rising trot.
Take up with your teacher any difficulties you may have.

Make an attempt to alter your own stirrup leathers; have the

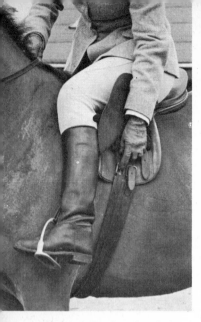

Above: Adjusting the girth: note the two buckles and the flap which the rider pulls down over them. The correct tightness of the girth is arrived at by common sense—would *you* feel comfortable with that pressure?
Below: Adjusting the stirrup leathers. Note that one hand only is used; the other holds the reins.

adjustment of the girth explained to you and get the feel of how tight it ought to be (it is often far too tight).

Mounted exercises

Before you actually go on to learn the aids, you will probably need to improve your balance in the saddle. So far you should have been holding the front arch of the saddle with both hands to help you to sit correctly; now you will hold firstly with one hand only, probably while working on some arm-circling exercises with the free arm and then you will let go with both hands, probably with more arm exercises.

Some instructors are very keen on 'mounted exercises' although, by and large, most adults feel rather silly waving their arms and legs about. I hope they will be kept to a minimum. They *can* be helpful in correcting certain stiffnesses, particularly when the rider is on the lunge. I also hope that they are used to correct particular faults, and are regarded as a means to an end and not as an end in themselves: e.g. arm circling to the rear helps the novice sit tall, deep in the saddle, with square but relaxed shoulders.

I will not mention any more because I don't suppose you will ever really *need* to do them. Too often, they are used as a time waster to give the horses a breather.

Controlling aids

Now is the time to start controlling the horse yourself; this can be done initially with the legs only, without using the reins at all, and it is good to practise this way. These changes of pace are called 'transitions'.

To go forward sit down and stretch the legs downwards; close the inside of the leg against the horse wherever it happens to be in contact. As the horse is shaped like a barrel your legs will not touch it all the way down—*do not try to make them.* Imagine you are wearing a pair of stockings with a seam down the back; the inside of the leg is the horse side of the seam. You close the legs in this way to go forward and also

25

Above left: Correct use of the rein: right rein leading the forehand to the right, a clear aid for right turn.
Above right: Incorrect use of right rein for turn—note the hand taken across horse's neck and therefore pulling back.
Below: Loose ends of rein should not lie on top of rein; it interferes with signals from hand to mouth.

to retrieve an existing rhythm should it be slowing. You increase the 'energy' or 'impulsion' of the horse; a good teacher will see any loss of rhythm and will encourage you to do this.

Do not kick with your heels: this is poetic licence!

You must be consistent in your aids or the horse will not know how to respond.

To slow down simply sit heavy in the saddle and again stretch down into your heels. Think of stopping; as you do so you automatically stop your body following the movement and this resistance is felt by the horse. He will respond to it even if you haven't yet used the reins.

Now, at last, you are in a fit state to pick up and hold the reins! You will not experience any great difficulties if you have first learned to sit still without the reins. It is a question now

'Pulling the horse up.' This is quite wrong; the reins are being used like a handbrake.

of co-ordinating the use of the legs and the hands—rather in the same way as you use the hand brake and clutch when starting your car on a hill. Because you are not yet expert at 'sitting in', adjusting automatically to the movement of the horse, you will not at first be able to keep a contact on the rein but will be taught to allow them to be light and loose. You are still, remember, using only the seat and legs to increase and decrease pace (fairly successfully, I hope). Gradually, now, follow these movements with the rein. Do not pull back; just stop the hand from moving; it no longer continues to follow the movement—it stops. This is so simple and basic but extremely important for all your future riding. The expression 'pull your horse up' is completely misleading (the bit is not used like a handbrake). To go forward use your leg and seat and ease the reins. You will find that at first there is a tendency to jerk the hands at the same time as you use the legs. Resist this. To turn left, lead the head to the left with the left rein; similarly for the right.

At all times the seat and legs work first; they are the important aids. Riders in general use the reins far too much and the seat and legs far too little.

There are now three more joints to add to the other shock absorbers—the elbow, wrist and fingers. In a walk the horse moves his head up and down, rather in the same way as we swing our arms; therefore the rider must soften the elbows and allow the hand to follow this movement. In a trot the horse's head remains almost still but the rider's body will be moving up and down with the trot rhythm; therefore the rider must use the shock-absorber joints to buffer this movement in order that the hand on the reins shall not move with the body. At all times the rider's hand follows the movement of the horse's mouth. The rider's hand must be divorced from the movements of his body.

I hope you are not burdened with detailed rein aids (signals) at this time (nor at any time, come to that, for signals given by the reins are, in fact, very simple). Neither need you be concerned with the type of bridle you use. All *you* need is one rein in each hand. It is up to the instructor to see that the bridle is of a suitable type—I do hope you are not given an incomprehensible lecture on bitting.

You may hear people talk about 'light hands'. This phrase *has* a meaning, as you will discover. If you think about it, you will see that this entire book is about 'light hands'. The point is that 'light hands' is not a thing in itself—it is a shorthand for good riding.

N.B. You will feel less apprehensive on your second visit to the school and more inclined to look about you. Notice the condition of your horse and of the others in the yard. The horses in a riding school are next in importance to the teacher. If they are uncared for it does not speak well for the instruction in general. See Appendix 1 for things to look for.

Stage Three
Ready for the 'open road'

After approximately two lessons you will be off the lunge, controlling the horse yourself. During the next two lessons you continue this process of controlling the horse through most of its different 'paces', becoming conversant with and understanding the basic controlling aids and adding to this fundamental 'vocabulary'.

Up to the end of this fourth lesson the tuition will be fairly concentrated and under the close direction of the instructor. You will have absorbed lots of advice and reached the stage where you can control a quiet horse under normal conditions. It will be a good plan then to ride out; this enhances your awareness; your horse will look about him and will be anxious to keep up with the others (herd instinct); he will quicken his step when you face toward home. Riding up and down hill, on hard roads and soft mud will increase your self reliance enormously. I hope you are near an area where there are bridle paths for these are obviously more fun.

The 'lesson three' setback

But there is still a long way to go before you will be ready for this. The first thing you must overcome is a feeling of frustration when, at about the beginning of lesson three, you join a class of other riders of similar standard, having previously had the advantage of learning on the lunge. In all probability a more advanced rider will be chosen to lead the ride. You will seem to make little or no progress and will find yourself just ready to start the lesson as it is coming to its end.

This is quite usual at this stage. The other riders will distract your attention, and your horse will be interested in the other horses; you will find your aids are not as good as they were and your horse does not seem to understand them. Do not be discouraged or apprehensive: your horse will most likely follow the others and you will have time to sort out your thoughts and make clearer aids. You will find that your position is not as good as it was; this is because the horse is no longer kept in regular rhythm by the instructor. Do not worry—you will soon be able to regain this yourself.

Do not think the horse is being cussed. He is a very simple creature—not intelligent but with a wonderful memory (much better than yours). He is by nature anxious to please and those who appear stubborn or lazy are generally just muddled and do not understand what is required.

By the fourth lesson you will feel quite at home working in a group with other horses and riders. You will not be so occupied with yourself, so inclined to fix your eyes on the horse's ears. Look about you. Do you know exactly where the other riders and horses are? At this stage all the horses used in the class will be quiet and agreeable but many horses are temperamental and sensitive and become nervous if another horse gets too close behind—perhaps kicking out. This is because the back of a horse's heel (like yours) is very tender; the animal in front is bound to be apprehensive of the one following and you should keep half a horse's length, about four feet, as the minimum distance. If you are asked to keep this distance, you will know that you are correctly spaced if

The 'rocking-horse' motion of the canter: as the forehand rises the rider rocks forward; with the forehand down the rider sits upright in the saddle.

you can just see the top of the tail of the horse in front of you. Not more. Look through your horse's ears.

It is easy to drift into a state of daze when on horseback. Keep your wits about you: look ahead to the ground where your horse is about to tread—even in a school or manège there may be iron jump-pegs half covered in shavings. Do not tread on them; call out to those behind; tell the instructor. Outside there may be a half-broken bottle; this could lame a horse for a month. If rabbits are around, look out for rabbit holes.

The canter

At this stage you will learn to canter. The first time you do it is the most exciting moment in all riding. It's a thrilling, rocking, three-time movement that you sit to—it feels great.

The motion is identical to that of the children's rocking horse: as the front end comes up the rider leans forward from the hip. Try this out now, sitting on a chair: keep your back quite flat and take your body forward from the hip, not moving your seat. As the front end goes down the rider returns to the normal upright position—try that. Nothing more is involved in maintaining your seat in a canter.

The best procedure, adopted in most schools, is for the teacher to make sure you are sitting well and then to command the horse to canter and catch up the rear of the ride. You will just get the feel of a few strides and then the horse will quietly return to the trot on his own. The first canter should not be a hectic performance of kicking, shouting and faster and faster trotting until it is finally achieved. In fact, at this stage you shouldn't be concerned with the aids at all. The instructor will control the horse; all you do is sit down, close both legs and ease the reins. You will notice that the horse is often asked for a canter as you go through a corner; this helps him strike off on the right leg.

The essential basic aids

By now you ought to be developing a sense of rhythm in your

Making the horse bend

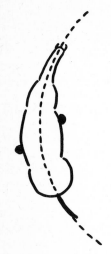

The correct bend.

The wrong bend.

Too much bend in the neck.

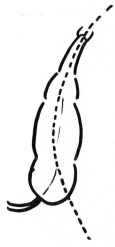

The quarters swinging out.

riding; with it will come the solution of most of your general difficulties. You will begin to be comfortable on a horse; you will be able to devote more attention to your aids.

Up to now you should have been riding in a fairly small area under the eye of your instructor; he can sort out difficulties as they arise and prevent the horse from getting out of control. Up to now, also, you have been using both legs together and both reins together; now is the time to develop the ability to use each leg and each rein for a particular purpose. When you have done this, you will have grasped the basic aids for every other movement you may wish to make, right up to advanced, high school movements. It is worth emphasising again and again that these aids are very simple and in no way mysterious.

The easiest way to understand these aids is to relate them to the circle. You have more or less been riding in a permanent circle because it is convenient to teach in this way. But the fact also has important implications. Every riding movement has an 'inside' and an 'outside'; these terms can best be explained by referring them to the circle.

The inside of a circle or corner is that nearest the centre; i.e. when circling or turning left the left leg is the inside leg. When you turn a corner on a bicycle, the inside edge of the tyre bites into the ground and provides most of the driving power. So with the horse: his inside hind leg is the worker. Therefore the rider's inside leg is the most vital; it must always be in the normal riding position, i.e. slightly behind the girth. From here it produces the driving power or 'impulsion' by stimulating the horse's inside hind leg.

As it does this, the inside leg is also helping with a second task, for as the horse's inside hind leg comes under, prompted by the rider, it promotes a bend in the horse's ribs and spine (a lengthbend). Obviously, to negotiate a circle or corner economically and well, the horse must bend his body to conform to the shape of the circle. The horse finds this bending difficult (or at least an effort) and so he tries to evade it and to keep his spine straight. The inside leg of the rider prompts him to bend.

So much for the inside leg. What of the rider's outside leg

35

on the circle? Well, the horse also tries to evade the lengthbend of his body by letting the outside hind leg swing outside the circle. To prevent this the rider's outside leg must be ready to move behind the girth and, by resisting against this side, say 'no'.

Do not try to lean inwards; try to sit level in the saddle.

Now the reins. You have already been using the inside rein to turn, taking it slightly to the inside (open rein) to lead the forehand in the direction required; this bends the head and neck. You must now think about the outside rein—what is this to do, if anything? This rein controls the pace of the horse; it must be kept very quiet, still, with the horse's mouth. Think of the horse as being rather like a fishing rod: the head and neck, being the thin end of the rod, away from the reel, will bend easily. But for the horse to conform to the shape of the circle the head and neck must not bend too much; the outside rein will prevent this happening.

You will not be able to put all this into practice at once but, if you think about it as you ride, it will come slowly.

Stage Four
Jumping

Provided you are sufficiently confident, there is no reason why you should not progress towards simple jumps during the fifth lesson, after suitable 'riding in', of course (this expression describes the warming up period for the horse, when he has just come out of his box and needs quiet riding and suppling up before work). How the jumping sequence is arranged varies from school to school. I will confine myself to general points of explanation. The understanding of what is happening and why you do particular things is of more importance than the nature and disposition of the obstacle you tackle.

What happens during jumping?

When riding on the flat you strive to make your legs long and allow your knee to sink as far below the widest part of the horse as possible—remember that a horse is barrel-shaped. You try to stay in contact with the saddle (by this I mean keep your *seat* in the saddle) so that you sit deep and heavy and use your seat both to produce impulsion and to slow down, and to feel rhythm and bend. You try to sit tall, with a long leg.

Not so long ago riders tried to jump like this and you can see pictures of them, sitting bolt upright over the fence; the poor horse has his head in the air and his mouth pulled painfully open. The rider, you see, had to hold on to the reins in order to stay in the saddle; if they broke he fell off backwards. Eventually an Italian named Caprilli realised that this was defying all the laws of forward movement; he pioneered the present style of jumping, which bears his name.

To understand the style, let us think about the horse. As he comes up to the fence he lowers head and neck to look at it and judge its size, then he brings his hocks under him and raises his forehand off the ground (the take off). He then stretches out to clear the width of the obstacle—now his head and neck stretch to the uttermost and the loin muscles hoist the hind legs over the fence (the flight). As the forelegs touch down, the head and neck start to come up again and, as the hind legs come down, the horse gets into his stride (landing).

The rider has to cope with the thrust of take off and the shock of landing. These must be absorbed in the hip, knee and ankle joints; in order to do this the rider shortens the stirrups and inclines the body forward, so closing the angle of the hip and knee. The rider now has simply to *maintain* this seat, sitting *still* and strong. He closes his knee and grips; the knee must remain bent but must not slide back on the saddle.

If you do all this and also make sure that your shoulder does not come in front of the knee, you are virtually there. Keep noting your shoulder position.

The horse needs freedom to move his head and neck and you will find it easier to follow his movements with your hand and arm if you are sitting forward and *still* as opposed to swinging forward and recovering. Therefore keep the shoulders still when increasing pace (not forward, in front of the knee) and avoid returning to an upright position when reducing pace. Keep your weight pressing down into the heel; weight

Above: Correct jumping position. Note the back is firm and the hand and arm are following the stretch of the head and neck to perfection.

Below: Incorrect jumping position—back collapsed, knee loose, rider's weight falling back on saddle, hand and arm restricting stretch of head and neck. Note the distress of the horse.

A stationary demonstration of the wrong jumping
position, with the shoulders in front of the knee.

Practising the jumping position by riding up and down a bank. Notice how the rider looks ahead and not down.

is taken on the inside of the thigh, the knee, down into the heel.

The best way to acquire a firm seat over fences is to ride with a shorter stirrup up and down hills and banks, not making any actual jumps (sand hills and dunes are ideal). Remember to keep forward both up and down hill; the uphill work is identical to the take off for a jump and the downhill to the landing. Your instructor need only explain how to sit, put you in position and make sure you maintain it; there is no need to have the reasons explained in detail.

Make sure you are *taught* how to jump, not just encouraged to 'have a go', learning to 'stick on' by trial and error. Too many instructors are satisfied and thankful if horse and rider reach the other side of the fence in one piece. You may enjoy this challenge but you will not progress quickly and the horse will not relish the thoughtless riding which must result. Do remember the horse.

Jumping should be a quiet, orderly procedure—not accompanied by shouts and chasing and cracking of whips.

Stage Five
Consolidation on the flat

You have now learnt all the basic things and it is time to get down to polishing and consolidating the different paces on the flat. You will now no longer be working entirely as a 'ride' (following one behind the other) but will be turning across the school or paddock and working in open order as individuals. At this stage, riding to music is a great help; it is particularly helpful to novice riders who find it difficult to keep a steady canter pace—a swinging waltz prevents it getting faster and faster.

A good instructor will have talked to you about the different paces as problems present themselves during the lessons. Let us look at the likely problems you have discussed, taking the paces in turn.

The walk

This is one of a horse's most precious possessions, for it is so easily lost. Few horses walk well yet they could all walk freely and regularly before we got on their backs. We have over-bustled and hurried them out of their regular beat; we have made them run in little short steps—no longer 1 . . . 2 . . . 3 . . . 4 . . . but 1.2 . . . . 3.4 . . . . All this while we imagined we

Walking on a loose rein; notice that the rider is allowing
the horse to stretch down, so fostering freedom of the loins
and length of stride.

were making them 'walk on well'. Or we may have neglected
to allow them to stretch their necks down on a long rein,
enabling their loins and hind quarters to swing along. We have
always kept a contact on the reins and have niggled with the
legs in a mistaken idea of keeping them active. This only
makes the horse stiff in the loins and shortens the stride.

Now then! The feet strike the ground near fore (near =left)
. . . off hind . . . off fore . . . near hind, or NF . . . OH . . . OF
. . . NH. The horse must track up otherwise the pace is not
true. What is 'tracking up'? A horse is tracking up when the
footprint left by the foreleg (i.e. NF) is completely covered by
the oncoming hind leg (i.e. NH). This shows that the horse is
propelling himself with the hind legs: they are coming well
under him. This affects even the novice, for the horse going
forward well is easy and pleasant to ride whereas the horse
going on his forehand is heavy, jerky and difficult to sit on.

Paces of the walk

Near hind.

Near fore.

Off hind.

Off fore.

46

I feel sure your instructor has already said to you 'Your horse is not tracking up—ride more forward', and you applied your legs and corrected the fault.

Try to make the stride free and athletic; if a horse is ridden correctly he will remain athletic into old age. This applies to all paces but to the walk most of all.

The trot

The rhythm will have been explained to you over and over again. Everyone trots too fast and so shortens the stride. Provided the horse is tracking up the rhythm cannot be too slow. The horse moves his legs in diagonal pairs: NF and OH (left diagonal) striking the ground together, followed by OF and NH (right diagonal).

Of the two sorts of trot, rising and sitting, it is the latter which will give most trouble. 'Sitting trot' is a term which I find misleading. The instructor generally means 'sit to the trot' or 'cease rising'; the trot should still be the ordinary trot, with no diminution of pace. As it is difficult for the novice to sit into an ordinary trot, most teachers allow and indeed encourage pupils to shorten the horse's stride, so that it actually ceases to be an ordinary trot. Remember this and, as you improve, see that you sit to a longer, springier stride. Otherwise the horse will be spoilt and you will miss a lot of fun.

To sum up: try to keep the same rhythm whether sitting or rising; avoid increasing pace when rising and decreasing when sitting.

N.B. Why 'ordinary' trot? You will have heard the phrase often and will have learnt the commands 'prepare to trot . . . ordinary trot, rising—t-e-e-rrrot(!) . . .' etc. Ordinary trot is mid-way between a collected trot and an extended trot; these are difficult exercises for a horse and will not concern a rider until he has two or three years' experience behind him.

Riding on a diagonal

When sitting to the ordinary trot your seat is coming into the saddle as each diagonal pair of legs strikes the ground. In the rising trot the seat comes into the saddle as one pair of legs strikes the ground and is out of the saddle as the other pair strikes; you are riding on the left diagonal if your seat comes into the saddle as the NF and OH strike the ground.

Changing Apart from developing a feel for the movement of the horse's legs, it is important for the horse that you ride for equal periods on each diagonal. If this is neglected the horse becomes one sided. To change diagonals you sit in the saddle for an extra beat before continuing to rise. It is generally accepted that when riding a circle it is most logical to ride on the outside diagonal. Your instructor must continue to remind you of this; he will say 'change the diagonal'.

The canter

Already you will have felt the three-time rhythm and you will know that the horse can canter in two ways—with the left legs leading, in 'left canter', or in 'right canter'. It is easier to understand the aids for canter if you understand the mechanics of the pace. If the horse is going away in left canter the first leg he moves is the OH; this is followed by the right diagonal and the last leg to hit the ground is the NF (Right canter—NH, left diagonal, OF).

You will now understand why the rider's right leg must be used just behind the girth, to stimulate the right hand leg to come forward and start off the canter sequence for left canter. Up to now the *horse* has been striking off into correct canter, that is with the inside legs leading, according to the direction

Paces of the canter

First step.

Second step.

Third step.

you were moving. If the horse made a mistake your instructor asked you to return to the trot and to strike off again, whereupon the horse corrected itself. Now you will be able to start asking the horse to strike off on whichever canter lead you require.

The gallop

You will find that this is the only mention of the gallop in this book and I confess that it is only included here for completeness. The reason is simple: the gallop is easy and obvious for the rider once he can do the other paces. To this is coupled the fact that the gallop is extremely tiring for the horse (it is his sprint) and that therefore you will do it seldom. If you want to gallop, make sure you are riding a fit, corn-fed horse.

Just as your car is of no value without an engine under the bonnet, neither is your horse of value unless the hind legs, the hocks, are really working. These are the power house, not the forelegs. Do not therefore become engrossed in the forehand (e.g. it is not strictly correct to say that a horse leads with the near fore leg; he leads with the near fore *and* near hind legs).

When striking off in canter avoid leaning forward to look at the foreleg. Keep upright and you will soon learn to feel the correct canter. It is disastrous to take your seat out just at the moment when you need it for pushing power.

Riding in between jumps

Never is it more important to remember all the above points about the different paces, than when you are jumping. There is a temptation to concentrate exclusively on the actual jump, neglecting the riding in between the obstacles. But this riding is the whole crux of the matter.

If you are to enjoy the good feel of a horse jumping under your will and control, with a free flowing and smooth action, never turning his head, exuding power and confidence, imbuing *you* with confidence; if you are to enjoy all these things, then you must do more than just point the horse at the fence and hope he will take you over to the other side. *You* must give the horse its confidence. Remember that he is not a natural jumper, though some individuals seem to love it. He will only feel confident at the jumps if he is properly ridden between them. Be just as particular about the bend and rhythm, etc. As a horse must be able to see the fence some time before he reaches it, you must turn into the fence with the correct bend. If you have not been taught to use your inside leg to achieve this, you will run into difficulties every time you come round a corner into a fence.

By now you should be riding for about twenty minutes in every hour in a jumping seat, even though you may not be jumping any fences.

Striking off into canter: do not lean forward to look
at the leading foreleg, as shown here.

The warning sign that all is not well is clear: you will quite
simply feel uncomfortable on the horse—you will be jolted
and jerked. *Always* remember this—not only when jumping.
Comfort when riding is the thing—that is why you spend all
this time learning to control the horse's impulsion, to maintain
rhythm, to make the horse bend in the shape of the circle or
corner. We do this in order to ride more *pleasantly* from point
A to point B, negotiating any obstacles in our path with the
least discomfort.

Stage Six
Riding out: keeping control

You may already have been out of the manège, riding in the larger area of the paddock, perhaps following in single file behind an assistant instructor, also mounted. You may have negotiated slopes—up and down—and rough patches of ground. You may also have trotted quietly down the road to help you learn the rise to the trot.

But you will only have made these excursions briefly. It is now time to put into practice all you have learnt and to ride out into the countryside. This is it, you will think, and rightly so: there is no more enjoyable way of seeing the countryside and enjoying the fresh air than from the back of a horse. This is why you are learning.

It may seem miserable of me, therefore, to pull you up short with a chapter almost entirely devoted to cautions but I think you will see that they are necessary. I closed the last chapter with the importance of continuing to ride well and intelligently when jumping. Now I repeat the same plea: do remember to ride well when out and about in the country-side for the first time. Think of the horse if you abandon all the carefully applied aids, kicking with the legs and tugging on the reins in a rough and ready fashion. How is he supposed to understand? Strange, muddled aids make no more sense to the horse than does someone talking to you in Outer Mongolian.

You will *need* to ride as well as possible, too, for you will have to concentrate on many new things, as you will see. Most of these are concerned, in one way or another, with maintaining control at all times over the horse. It surprises many novices how quickly a horse will sense that his rider is not quite in command and riding out can give the horse many opportunities to take over control. This chapter is largely devoted to forestalling this.

Road sense

As you will learn, not only motorists drive irresponsibly; there are many times when I wonder why more horses and riders are not injured in traffic. Remember that most motorists do not realise that a horse may step sideways into his path (e.g. if a cow suddenly pops her head through the hedge). The image of the 'toffee-nosed' horseman dies hard: acknowledge good manners from a car, lorry or bus, even if their courtesy was barely or grudgingly given; you may encourage them to do better next time! If you happen to be at the rear of a file of horses, wave traffic on. It depends on the width of the road, whether you ride in single file or not; if your horse is not 100% quiet, arrange for a quiet horse to pair with you on the outside.

If, at a later date your own horse is really jumpy at traffic, don't hesitate to stop it firmly—better a dirty look than an accident. Don't turn back from anything the horse dislikes; either dismount and walk him by or turn aside into a lane, as though that is what you intended all the time. The horse learns by association, remember.

Setting the pace

If you find yourself at the front of the ride, remember to set what may seem an exaggeratedly slow and regular pace, for invariably the horses at the rear move faster than the leaders. This must be controlled: apart from the damage done to their legs from banging on the hard road, the horses think they are

54

being left behind, become excited, and the novice may lose control. This can happen suddenly: the horse may make an excuse to shy at something and break into a canter; on a hard, slippery road this is dangerous.

All this is even more important if, due to the lack of bridle paths, etc., the major part of the ride takes place on road; it must then be accepted that the ride must trot on while actually on the road.

All horses enjoy working on soft ground: it gives them much the same feeling you have when, on a hot summer's day, you push your bare toes through the cool grass. Anticipate, therefore, that your horse will wish to become more energetic when you leave the road; walk him quietly to start with—control him. (It must happen, too, that the horse knows where it is customary to trot or canter along the route, which he probably knows well. Don't worry—he'll slow down soon for the same reason.) You are unlikely to have these problems on bridle paths, for the horses follow in single file; there is no possibility of overtaking and the whole thing developing into a free-for-all.

This control is the reason too (don't be too impatient, therefore) that your instructor moves you off in single file, and at a walk, when you first move out into an open space. It is, in fact, the reason behind most of the apparently odd practices which instructors seem to love! Cantering, for example, may be introduced on a convenient bridle path but if this is not possible and it has to be a field, note that the instructor will choose a field with an *uphill* slope and a guiding hedge pointing *away* from home. He will probably send the assistant and one pupil (possibly riding the most impetuous horse) to a point at the end of the field (not too far) and the rest of the ride will be sent off one by one; the horses will all stop on reaching the waiting group.

Do remember that although *you* may be under perfect control and longing to canter on, others on the ride may be riding young horses or be less proficient than you. Do not overtake, for example, for this excites the horse you are overtaking.

A ride negotiating a gate: the leaders wait when through.

Note the sideways on position of the gate-opener.

Caution in overtaking is, in fact, a general rule when riding. Rule is perhaps not the right word—it is good manners really. Everyone knows it can be dodgy so they behave with due prudence. There are, of course, those breathtaking moments when your horse takes over and decides what to do—and you really cannot help overtaking!

If you are ever overtaken on your horse, have a regard for him; galloping sounds, etc. from behind disturb and frighten him. Stop and turn the horse toward the sounds, so that he can see them coming.

If, at this stage you are nervous, do not clutch at the reins and tighten up in the saddle; this conveys excitement to the horse. It is as though an adult were to keep repeating 'Don't be afraid' in a high-pitched voice to a small child, nervous of the dark. It will only make the child more afraid.

Gates and jumps

The need to keep control governs the procedure whereby a rider negotiates a gate: the leader rides his horse up beside the gate, facing the catch, opens the gate and stands holding it while the rest walk through, leaving space for those following and waiting. The leader then pivots round the gate, pulling it closed and fastening the catch. Only then will the ride continue. Why this rigmarole? Gates must be closed and it is difficult to keep a horse quietly against the gate in order to fasten it while all the other horses are moving away out of sight.

Similarly when jumping: if the instructor indicates a small tree trunk, ditch or gap in the hedge, wait your turn, do not follow too closely (the horse in front may stop or run out) and, having jumped the fence, wait quietly. Do not canter away as this will make the horses behind rush the fence.

N.B. Sometimes it is quite impossible to open a gate without dismounting (or you may notice a broken bottle in a dangerous place). On these occasions it is helpful if another rider holds your horse. Dismount, run up the stirrup irons and take the reins over the horse's head; lead the horse up on the right of the other rider and hand over the reins. He must hold the horse sensibly (horses, like people, have friends and enemies; mares in particular like nipping and threatening to kick another horse). He transfers the stick and reins into the left hand and holds the reins about 18 inches from the bit so that the horse's head is level with the knee. The horse's head must be turned inward and the quarters kept away.

Controlling the shying horse

You will have noticed that a horse disregards a huge articulated lorry as it passes by and yet stops and pricks up its ears at a piece of newspaper blowing in the gutter. All the usual things he ignores; sudden movements—a dog running down the garden path and barking at the gate—cause him to shy. A cyclist wearing an oilskin cape that makes a crackling noise frightens him more than a double-decker bus.

Leading a horse; when stationary, keep the lead horse facing you and don't let it get behind your own mount.

I can remember riding on the beach during the war, escorting ponies ridden by schoolboys. Two planes zoomed over us so low that they whisked off all our hats and my hairnet. The ponies didn't move a muscle!

The horse you are riding at this stage should be pretty well shy proof but the unforeseen does occur. If you feel he is going to shy at that plastic bag rattling in the hedge bottom to your right, turn his head to the left so that he cannot look at it. Your right rein now becomes the outside rein and will prevent him dashing forward. Your left leg (inside leg) is working hard on the girth, keeping the left bend and the horse moving forward (not backing up and moving sideways into the middle of the road). Your right is behind the girth, holding the quarters.

Later on you will learn that this is the 'shoulder in' movement—a rather clumsy name for the most useful manoeuvre for the novice rider and horse.

Homeward bound

All horses have an inbuilt compass and, given the opportunity, will find their way back to the stable; when you turn for home your horse knows it and will consequently quicken his step. No good horseman turns for home and bursts abruptly into an exuberant canter—if the procedure is repeated the horse becomes so 'hotted up' and excitable that after six months of the treatment he is unridable. Vary the places where you turn for home; make sure the horse is walking or quietly trotting; walk the last half mile or so to prevent the horse dashing into the stable yard. If the ride has been well run it is unlikely that the horse will be hot but after a long ride on a hot day or a strenuous ride in winter, when the horse may have a long coat, you may find he is sweating and needs to cool off. If you have the girths very tight, as you may if you have been riding in hill country, it is a good idea to loosen them a hole to allow the horse to relax and cool off as you walk in.

Shying and how to correct it—turn the horse's head
so that he won't see the distraction.

Stage Seven
Working the horse

All the preceding pages have been aimed at providing you with the foundation for competent riding. This can be put very simply: a firm and supple seat, completely independent of the reins and so relaxed that it is maintained without effort, by sitting in and blending with the movement of the horse.

This procedure has been essentially passive, i.e. learning to react and adapt to the movements of the horse. It has been a process of correction to your position and development of your seat. You have been adapting to the horse; now is the time to turn the tables and take over from him. You have acquired a reasonably sound seat; now is the time to use it positively, make the horse do what you want. Instead of just sitting on and guiding the animal in the required direction, start to ask for more energy, begin to produce the horse so that he performs to the best of his ability.

Going forward from the leg

We have used the word 'impulsion' and pointed out it was another word for energy. Where does it come from? The horse produces it mainly in the hocks, as the hind legs come forward under the horse; the hocks and joints of the quarters bend and allow the horse to 'sit down' and then propel it forward slowly and springily. It follows that when we use the legs, the horse should not tip on its forehand and run on but should step under with the hind leg and push itself forward. *Think* of it in this way—the pushing movement coming from behind.

Do not confuse impulsion with speed; your car in top gear at 60 m.p.h. has less impulsion, less r.p.m., than when in bottom gear climbing a hill. 'Impulsion' is energy, springiness at the joints, buoyancy. When you hit a horse with a whip, so that it jumps forward, you are *not* providing impulsion.

Rhythm

Concentrate on this as you ride. Each horse must be ridden to a slightly different rhythm. If the stride is short it is easy to ride in too fast a rhythm, making the horse tip on its forehand and hurry in quicker and shorter strides. If the horse has a long stride it is important to make sure the horse goes on enough, particularly in canter, so that he tracks up and completes his natural stride. As you get stronger in the saddle, ask the horse to be more energetic in the hind legs, to bring them under; this will slow down the rhythm without shortening the stride. As you are now riding with more impulsion, the horse will spring more, challenging your ability to sit. *This is as it should be*: master the difficulty, do not ease off (see *Accepting the bit* below).

Accepting the bit

There is confusion about the way a horse should go, particularly its general outline or shape, and the feel a rider should have. Most beginners say that the head should be high; this means that the back, where the rider sits, sinks down and the hind legs fall behind. The rider would sit in a hollow and feel no movement. *It is quite wrong.*

63

Think of the shape of the horse when jumping—he is rounded, his back basculed, and he moves through a parabola. This is the shape he should maintain in all his paces. He must be supple, springy and rounded through his whole spine, from head to tail and down through his hind legs. The hind legs come under, the horse bends through the length of his spine and his head stretches down, seeking the rider's hand and accepting the bit.

You must learn to sit this springy stride, this superb feel of power. Think about it; feel it; encourage it. 'Stretching down to seek the bit'—a lovely phrase.

Bend

Most horses like to bend to the left and find it more difficult to bend to the right. You must feel which way your horse likes to bend, which is his good side. Just as a man knows the feel of his car, knows when the engine is running sweetly; just as a woman tests the feel of silk or wool with her fingers, so you must now assess your horse. You cannot ride every animal the same; one who bends well to the left will not be ridden in quite the same way as one who bends to the right.

Prevent the horse bending too much the good way by using the outside leg and rein to correct this. When bending the bad way, insist with the inside leg that the hind leg steps further forward, bend the neck and head in the required direction with the inside rein, stop the quarters from swinging with the outside leg and rein; you will have produced the bend you require.

Remember to keep the rhythm by riding ever forward when changing direction.

Changing horses

The time will come when you are given a different horse to

ride—different in size and temperament. Instead of a nice, square, solid sort of cob (very much a starter's horse) you may find yourself on something narrow, possibly rather thin-skinned and sensitive. Assess the new horse. Jolly, cheery, rather plump people generally need chivvying along and they take it all in good heart; thin, nervous people need to be carefully led. It is the same with the horses you ride.

A keen horse that needs little pushing helps you to sit still and to get the feel of jumping. But to develop a strong seat and power in your legs, you must ride the lazy ones that need pushing. If you start on a lazy horse you are probably a bit too 'busy'; a keen horse will teach you to sit still (if you do not then he will soon be dashing away with you).

Working a horse on your own

Different pupils have different problems; common tuition is often impractical at this stage. You will now, of necessity, be left more to your own devices and must work the horse on your own. Initially, novice riders cannot think of any programme: all they can think to do is canter and, of course, the horses soon tire and difficulties start.

It is a big step forward in your riding and will tax your ability to assess your horse. First you must ride him in quietly, without asking him any serious question; try a longer rein to allow him to stretch down his head and neck, and loosen up his back and loin muscles.

Next, having found out his good rein—discovered to which side he prefers to bed—work him in large, 20 metre circles trying to achieve a good rhythm and developing a soft swinging stride. Your ever watchful instructor may call out to you when it is 'well done', but you ought to be able to tell yourself, by the smooth feel of the ride.

Once you have the horse going as well as you can on a good rein, change to the difficult rein and try keeping the same rhythm and relaxed swinging stride. You will need to use a much more active inside leg to achieve the bend: your horse will try to evade it by swinging his quarters out (and your

65

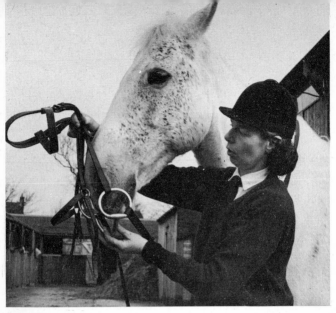

Bridling
Above: Grasp the bridle by the cheek straps with the right hand which also steadies the horse's head.
Below: Open the mouth by pressing the fingers of the left hand on the bars, without banging the bit on the teeth. Guide it into the mouth with the thumb.

Bridling—*continued*
Above: Lift the headpiece high over the ears and see that the mane is lying straight.
Below: Fasten throat lash, nose bands, etc.; see all keepers are in place.

outside leg must be in place and ready to say 'no') and by trying to run away from your leg by increasing pace (your outside rein must be ready to prevent this).

If you are pleased with the trot on the difficult rein, walk with a long rein to reward and rest the horse. If you feel that you did not get a very good result, change back to the good rein and, after regaining a good trot, walk and relax. The reason for this is important but not obvious. It is 'psychologically' bad to allow the horse to relax after a difficult session, so give him a chance to do well again and let him relax with successful manoeuvres on his mind.

Break up the concentration for both yourself and the horse by some work in canter. Really enjoy this and let it be fun.

Now try some transitions. Work in trot and do not rise but sit to the trot; make the horse understand your slowing down aids using less and less rein—until you can get from trot to walk and from walk to halt simply by sitting deep in your seat, and stretching down into your heel. Once your horse can understand this, it is obviously much more pleasant for him, than having you using the reins.

You will now have much more feel. You will notice that very few horses will halt straight: one hind leg—always the same one—will swing out to the side. As yet you will not be able to feel this as it is actually happening but once you are in the halt you will notice that the quarters have swung sideways, say to the right. It is wrong simply to take the right leg back and push the quarters into line again. A new fault will develop—the horse will swing his quarters both ways—rather like the rumba. To correct this properly move on forward and halt again; but this time close the right hand and take it a little to the right and have your right leg ready to say 'no' if you feel the quarters pushing out against you.

A propos the above, never move the quarters to straighten a horse; always move the forehand over.

Another of your faults may be tipping forward when changing pace. Work on this by sitting deep in the saddle, and stretching down into the heel. Remember also that it is a good idea to ride in a jumping position for twenty minutes in every hour (where your body *is* inclined forward!).

The above faults may not apply to you. The important thing is to understand what is going wrong and practise putting it right. You cannot learn by going over the things you can already do.

These are the things you may well be doing while the instructor is attending to other people. General tuition will not cease, of course; your instructor will not desert you. It is a good idea to end a lesson with some jumping and a popular exercise, which he may arrange, is to put up a simple pole, 18 in. high, and, 18 to 20 ft. away from it, parallel bars, 2 ft. 6 in. high and 2 ft. 6 in. to 3 ft. apart. The horse will jump the first pole from a trot, make one canter stride and be exactly right for the second jump. Each jump will be symmetrical, the horse never standing back, never flattening, never getting too close to the fence, never having to jump up like a lift. The rider feels good because he knows that the horse will be right every time; he can concentrate on folding to the jump, on strengthening the lower leg position by anchoring the heel and not allowing it to swing, and on learning to follow the movement of the head and neck with an elastic arm. You will really feel you are making great strides by the end of this exercise.

Stage Eight
Straightening the horse

You will now be riding as individuals in open order, no longer as a rider keeping distance, but turning away into a space if you find yourself getting too close to another rider. In this way each rider can work his horse in the rhythm to suit that particular horse. He does not have to conform to the rhythm of the leader of the ride. At this stage it is still advisable to ride on the same rein—otherwise collisions occur. This means that some riders will have to start on the bad rein, i.e. work on their horse's stiff side, which is a drawback.

The task of keeping the horse straight at all times is the last major task you will have before attaining reasonable proficiency. In fact it is only because you are reasonably proficient that you are able to recognise and understand this problem.

The horse must be kept on a straight line—this is comparatively easy to follow when actually going straight but he must also be straight through a corner or a circle. Remember what this means: the hind legs should follow in the same path as the forelegs; if they swing out sideways then the horse has escaped your control and the impulsion is escaping, too. It is uneconomic. All instructors spend some part of every lesson watching their riders from behind or from the front, ready to point out any crookedness.

Avoid using the outside rein to hold your horse to the out-side of the circle or manège, as this turns the head out and throws the quarters in. Try to ride the horse out with the inside leg.

Work on the canter will continue, for there are very few horses that are quite straight at this pace. With novice riders, many horses carry their quarters to the inside when cantering to a circle—and bad habits take root! You will find it most helpful if the school has a mirror in which you can see your-self cantering. Then at least you can see what you ought to be feeling!

Chronic crookedness

Many horses carry their quarters to the inside because the rider has used too much rein and this has shortened the stride. The horse is not yet supple enough in the back, or strong enough in the quarters to bring the hind legs forward under the body, so he is forced to swing them to the side.

The correction for this is fairly straightforward: allow the horse to lengthen the stride by lightening the hand and following the stretching movement of the head and neck; make sure your inside leg is in place and is asking the horse to go forward.

However, if the horse habitually carries his quarters to the inside, the correction must be more specific. You must not move the quarters but must rather lead the forehand over in front of the hindlegs, with the inside rein; the outside rein has to work too, because the neck must not bend. The inside leg works hard and keeps the horse going forward; the outside leg prevents the body curling round too much and, lying behind the girth, it continues to say 'keep in right/left canter' (it would be a bad mistake if the horse became confused and tried to change the canter).

Once again, without realising it, you have ridden 'shoulder in', the movement you used to correct the shying horse.

Stage Nine
What next?

The tuition I have outlined represents a total of about 24 riding hours. You have covered the basics and have a good sound foundation. I suggest you stay with your original instructor until you have thoroughly mastered his tuition; if you want to ride elsewhere (e.g. on holiday) ask him to recommend a school that will teach along the same lines. It is too easy to be confused at this stage by seemingly different methods; in another year you will enjoy comparing methods and finding the one that seems to make the most sense.

Continue to broaden your experience, riding more difficult horses both inside and outside the paddock. Jump horses that need strong riding, that always refuse with novice riders. Progress to a young horse: at first this will be a shattering experience—he will not seem to respond and you will feel as though your seat has deteriorated.

The rider's world

You will be delighted at the prospects. As life speeds up and we travel ever faster and faster, we naturally mourn the loss of those best things from the past—the flickering fire in the hearth, the smell of baking bread. Perhaps this is the reason why people turn back to the horse; whatever it is, the fact is that they are taking up riding in ever increasing numbers and councils are continually being asked to provide more facilities.

In order to satisfy these demands of the riding public, there has arisen the Riding Club movement, one of its objects being to help and encourage the weekend rider. As in all clubs, most of the organisation and work falls on the shoulders of an energetic few—so all new members are welcome (particularly non-horse owners, who have more time to help). You can generally borrow mounts from your usual school and take part in instructional rallies, long rides and suitable competitions. Most clubs divide their activities into grades: novice, intermediate and open, so that no rider need feel outclassed.

The Prix Caprilli competition is especially designed for beginners and consists of riding a few circles in trot and canter, and jumping two small jumps, 2 ft. high. Marks are awarded for good riding and correct use of the aids. (One of the advantages of this competition is that riding-school horses are not at a disadvantage with respect to private horses. This is not always the case—in jumping events, for example, where they may become confused.) During winter, clubs may arrange for well-known personalities to give lecture/demonstrations with their horse at a local indoor riding school. Film shows and talks, quizzes and brain trusts are popular.

Some of the other riders from your school are sure to be members and probably the instructor teaches at some of the rallies but if you have any difficulty in locating one, write to the Riding Club's secretary: Miss Mary Martin Hurst, National Equestrian Centre, Stoneleigh, Warwickshire.

If you are not yet twenty-one, you may prefer to join the Pony Club, which is really a unique and excellent Youth Club. It is to every rider's advantage to join either of these organisations since, apart from providing you with a great deal of fun, they also look after all horsey interests, such as the prevention of bridle-path closures.

Some schools are also livery stables and during the winter

season there may be a number of horses kept in condition for their owners to hunt; you will be encouraged to have a day's hunting when your pocket allows and there is a suitable meet. Your hunter will cost about 5 gns for the day and the 'cap' (fee you pay the Hunt) may be from 3 to 10 gns. Your instructor will see you are suitably mounted and carefully escorted.

In summer you can go to local horse shows and you will soon get to know the riders and will enjoy comparing their merits and spotting their mistakes. Any offers of help you make will be gratefully accepted—as groom or jump steward, etc.

But actual riding is the thing, of course, and here no advice or encouragement will be needed from me: the more you ride the more you will want to ride; there is always something more to enjoy, something challenging round the corner. You can ride in Wales, the Yorkshire Dales and many parts of Scotland; there are the pony-trekking centres for holidays. You can organise your own tours—as my sister and I used to do in the Cleveland hills and the Esk Valley above Whitby. There will always be encouragement from schools and clubs.

The countryside will 'belong' to you as it belongs to few others.

Appendix One
Stable management window

You may wish to look through this window for two reasons. Primarily to give yourself an idea of what you yourself would be involved in if you decided to keep your own horse. Secondly to judge whether your school or centre is up to the mark. By and large you can accept that if the stables are run in a slip-shod manner, your lessons will also be slip-shod.

Condition of the horses

Are they clean, with mane and tail neatly brushed? There is no excuse for yellow stable stains, though if the horses have worked on the previous ride, they may have mud splashes, etc.

Are the horses all fat? Every riding school mount (and yours when you get it) should be well-covered in flesh. His life is a regular one and he works at a slow pace, not being asked to gallop or canter long distances. He should not be fit and finely tuned like a racehorse, which (as you see them at meetings) carries no spare flesh—just muscle. The horse you ride should not be short of fat: if you can count his ribs or if his hip-bones are prominent, he is not in good condition. He most probably needs more hay and more boiled barley. If you are paying fees of 17/6 plus for a class lesson of one hour, this should not be the case.

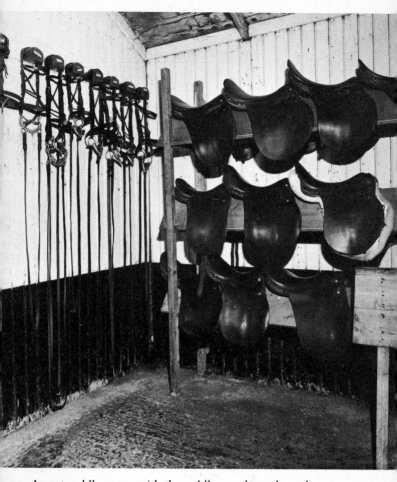

A neat saddle room, with the saddles on the racks and
the bridles hanging straight on wide bridle pegs.

The saddle room and saddlery

Have a look at the saddle room; in most schools these are kept beautifully. The bridles all hang neatly with the reins looped up so that they are not trailing on the floor; the saddles are carefully placed on the racks. This is the place where the stable staff spend many hours each week, cleaning, soaping and oiling the saddlery.

Look at the saddle and bridle on your horse. Is the leather soft and well-oiled? Are the metal parts polished? On damp days any metal will look dull but it should not be permanently marked or green with verdigris. The leather too may have surface grease and mud splashes but it should not be dull, blackened and hard. All the bridle ends should be tucked into the keepers; they should give the impression of fitting and should not pinch or rub.

Lift the flap of the saddle and check that the girth is flat (not twisted) and strong. There must be two buckles—it would be risky to ride with one. Girths are made with single buckles but they are worn in pairs, i.e. two buckles means two girths. The flap of the saddle should be protected from the pointed tongue of the buckles by a guard buckle—a small flap of leather.

Care of saddlery

It is dangerous to ride in 'tack' that has not been well cared for: the straps to which the girths are fastened are stitched high under the panel of the saddle and the stitching and the webbing to which they are fastened rot and may snap without warning as the horse rises to a jump—very nasty, believe me! This and other stitching need constant checking and regular repair.

Stirrup leathers that are left permanently on the saddle, always in the same fold, will one day crack at just the same sort of moment. The holes in the leathers are the points of weakness: they rub into a split which travels across the leather. (N.B. It is important that the stirrup leathers are up to your weight.)

The bridle is less vulnerable on the whole because it takes less strain but the reins are a danger point at the point where they join the bit. Here they are permanently bent around, and often wet and dirty with saliva. Stitching rots or they crack. Was it Grackle who lost the Grand National because his rein broke?

Regular cleaning is needed—ideally each day but at least twice a week if in daily use. A wipe-over is insufficient. Take the leathers and girths off the saddles and undo all straps on the bridle as far back as the buckle. Clean with a damp sponge. Rub on glycerine soap, feeding especially the undersides of the leathers and emphasising the danger points. Always check and recheck stitching, etc.

Try to hang it all up so that most of the leather hangs straight. Take girths and leathers off the saddle (stripping). Make sure that the bridle peg is wide, otherwise a 'poke' will develop in the headpiece (top of the bridle); make sure that the saddle rack is not sharp and likely to rip the underside of the saddle; make sure that the saddle will sit on it safely.

Two final points: remember that saddlery is valuable and don't invite thieves to pinch it; during wet weather leather needs low heat to prevent mould.

Fitting of the saddle

It should not press on the horse's spine; if it does it will be extremely uncomfortable as soon as you put your weight on it. By the end of an hour's work the back will be rubbed sore and a tired horse will start to stumble and may come down on his knees.

You can easily test this for yourself. When you have mounted, put four fingers of one hand under the front arch of the saddle, then stand up in the stirrups; if your fingers are pinched, tell the instructor that you think the saddle is down on the withers (that part of the spine joining the base of the neck to the back). A worthwhile instructor, knowing this is serious, will check this at once and put on either a wither pad or a numnah; this should be half an inch thick

A saddle pressing down on the withers (no room for
the fingers). A wither pad used as temporary protection.

to be of any use. Similarly test the back (or cantle) of the saddle
—fingers under and then sit heavily near to the cantle.

Good saddle design

A correct saddle will put the rider in the right place; it is as
beneficial to the horse as the rider. A good test is to place
your stick across the saddle from front to rear, resting on the
pommel and the cantle. The stick should be level: if the stick
is lower at the back then the rider will continually find himself sliding in that direction (no doubt bringing corrections
from the instructor about which he can do nothing!). There
should be a good dip in the centre of the saddle, showing
space under the stick. The flap should be shaped forward to
make a place for your knee; if there is a roll of padding (knee
roll) edging the flap, it will give you a firmer feel.

A well designed saddle, plus sound stirrup leathers, stainless steel stirrup irons and nylon or leather girths, costs from
£40 to £50. It is worth going to the expense of stainless
steel irons; they will never bend and trap a rider's foot as will
the softer, nickel irons.

Shoeing

A horse's foot, like your nails, grows continuously. Under
natural conditions it would wear itself level and keep itself
in sound condition. Today the hoof cannot keep pace with the
wear and tear of metalled roads, grit and the weight it has to
carry. Hence horseshoes.

But of course the horn still grows and so, after four or five
weeks, the toe is too long and the shoe is pulled forward out
of place. In this condition the horse is likely to stub his toe
and come down on his knees. Therefore he must visit the
farrier regularly to have the shoes taken off, the hoof cut back
and, after reshaping, the shoes put back. This operation goes
by the strange name of a 'remove'. If the horse has been working on the roads he will have worn down a set of shoes in
about three weeks and in this case will have a new set earlier.

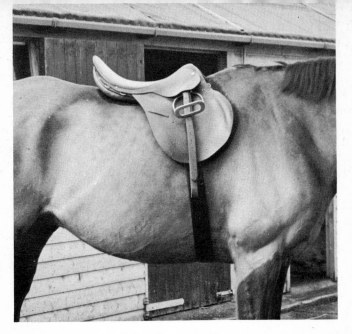

A correctly fitting saddle, of a good, all-purpose pattern.

Do your horse's feet look well shod? The ends of the nails come through the wall of the hoof and are turned over to help keep the shoe firm—they are called clenches. Are these sticking up—called a risen clench? Do the shoes sound loose? Worst of all—has the horse lost a shoe (listen for the quiet beat of the unshod foot)? Is the horn cracked or broken?

Boots and bandages

The feet and legs of a horse are all important and it is not only in shoeing that we manifest our concern for these regions.

Brushing boots The inside of the fetlock joint (ankle) can get kicked by the iron shoe of the other leg. To protect them from 'brushing' themselves in this way, we equip them with padded leather or felt boots, buckled round the leg below the knee or

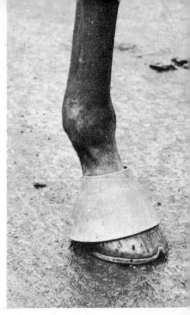

Above left: Brushing boots.
Above right: Over-reach boot
Below: Exercising bandage.

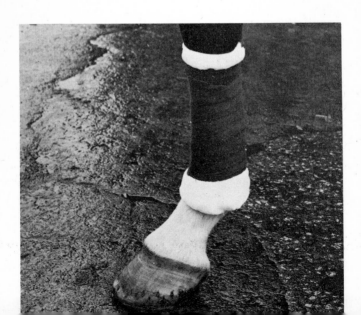

hock and overlapping down the inside of the fetlock joint. Many riding-school horses need brushing boots because unsteady, novice riders shift their weight in the saddle, causing momentary unbalance. Polo ponies wear boots as they are continually making quick, sharp turns.

Over-reach boots They look rather like goloshes and are pulled on over the hoof to protect the back of the heel. The majority of show-jumpers wear them, for the extra effort over a big fence can cause them to step on their own heels as they land.

Exercising bandages You may have noticed horses wearing bandages while racing or show-jumping, generally on the forelegs only but sometimes all round. These are known as exercising bandages; their function is to support the leg, rather in the nature of a wrist strap. It is important that a layer of padding (gamgee tissue) is placed round the leg, without creases and large enough to extend above and below the bandage; this prevents the edges cutting into the leg. The crepe bandage is then wound firmly and with even pressure from below the knee to above the fetlock (ankle joint).

Do not bandage your horse unless it is really necessary; grit finds its way under them, mud and wet makes them heavy.

They must only be used for the period of work and then removed; you then rub the leg to promote circulation.

Stable bandages You may have seen horses wearing thick woollen bandages all round when in transportation, etc. The horse, like us, suffers from poorer circulation in the legs than elsewhere and these 'stable bandages' are to keep them warm after heavy exertion or when standing still for a long time (e.g. a journey). They also protect the legs against knocks.

A good thick bed and a contented horse.

Gamgee tissue is laid under the lightly wrapped woollen bandage.

Bedding

Good bedding in the daytime is essential for the horse's well-being. They like to lie down during the day, particularly if it is sunny. If, in summer, the horse is out in the field at night and comes in to the stable during the day, he is even more anxious to lie down because he will have spent the night walking and feeding. Some horses, in fact, are so keen to take the weight off their legs that they will scrape a few bits of straw together and lie down on them, bruising themselves. Now, horses do not like to stale (spend a penny) if the urine is going to splash up on to their legs, which it will do if there is no bedding They *don't* stale and this makes them ill. Bad bedding is cruel, in fact.

A horse's daily ration, comprising 14 lb. hay, 3 lb. bruised oats, a handful of linseed, 2 lb. horse nuts, 4 lb. bran and a handful of chop.

A straw bed should be deep and springy, covering the whole box or stall, and banked up at the sides; it should tempt you to lie down in it! This straw is not an expensive luxury for the horse—in the long run it is a very decided economy. If you put down a good bed and look after it, the horse will stay fat because he is relaxed and warm and he will need less food because he is not using it to keep himself warm, or wasting it by nervously pacing the box. Most important of all— the more a horse lies down and takes the weight off his legs the longer he will last (just like the good servicing of a car, in fact—it's cheaper in the long run). Altogether, inadequate bedding means bad stabling.

As for droppings—there is an old saying that one pile is excusable, two are bad, three a disgrace. Every good stable should have a supply of skeps; they are made of rubber and it takes no time at all to remove the droppings with one.

Ready for travelling: note tail guard and padding on horse's
head. This protects the poll—it's dangerous if the
horse strikes himself there.

Clothing

In winter horses grow a thick coat, consisting of long hair on
the outside, to allow the rain to drain, and a short undercoat,
with extra grease secreted to withstand wind and water.
Working a horse with this thick overcoat causes stress and
sweating, so most are clipped. The following clothes are
used to replace the insulation at such times as it is needed.
As with bedding (see above) good, sufficient clothing is an
economy in the long run.

At night they wear one or two blankets and, on top of
these, a night rug, lined with wool and made of jute (sacking).
If a horse travels, the night rug is replaced by a day rug.
Sometimes horses are trace clipped or blanket clipped, when
the legs are left alone. They may then be turned out for
exercise in a green waterproof rug called a New Zealand rug.

A sweat rug is exactly like a string vest and is useful for a horse that is excitable and, although cool when brought into the stable, breaks out into a cold sweat after being rugged up. Horses suffer from flies and summer sheets, light linen checked rugs, protect them; they must have a fillet string round the tail to prevent the wind blowing it up and over the head, causing panic.

A last word: make sure your roller or surcingle is well padded and is not pressing on the spine. If it sinks down it will give the horse a sore back. You can use a piece of sacking as a temporary measure.

Grooming

WHY IS IT NECESSARY? Horses in their natural state live on grass and herbs. They keep their coat in condition by rolling on grass and in wet mud, letting it dry and then shaking and rolling it out (or they simply roll in sand). They rid themselves of loose hair at the time of changing coat, by rubbing on posts, etc.

Now we require the horse to work, so he is given more concentrated diet, is kept in the stable and generally clothed in rugs. The concentrated food adds to the secretions and the restriction on rolling inhibits the loss of hair. The more the horse is stabled, etc. the more grooming he needs; horses that are kept out in the field must not be so thoroughly groomed as this removes too much of that grease which acts as his natural mackintosh.

What is involved Firstly, in the morning, before work, the horse is given a quick brush over, the mane and tail are tidied by laying (flattened down by brushing the top with a water brush) and the hooves are picked out. This quick grooming takes 10 minutes and is called 'quartering'. The horse is given his thorough grooming, known as 'strapping', immediately after exercise, if possible. Then the pores are open and the natural oils have been secreted. Thus the coat can be more

Grooming kit. This comprises bucket, stable rubber,
sponge, rubber carry comb, wisp, scissors and mane comb,
dandy brush, hoof oil and brush, tail bandage, hoof pick,
body brush, carry comb and water brush.

thoroughly cleaned. It takes about 45 minutes for an expert
and it is hard work.

There is a saying that a good strapping is equal to a good
feed. This refers to wisping, which is a vigorous massage
given with a pad of hay or folded linen (like a tea towel).
This is brought down hard on all the muscular parts of the
horse, stimulating the oil glands (to give a shine) and toning
up the muscles.

The sweating horse   By and large this problem can be avoided
by walking the horse for the last 10 minutes of his outing.
But there are occasions when this is not sufficient, particularly
in winter, when the horse has a long coat. In this case, if he is
stabled, dry him well with a handful of straw and then put on

a sweat rug (or 'thatch' him—lay straw on his back and throw the rug on his back, inside out). The resulting air space enables the coat to dry off. If he lives in a field, this is not necessary as he walks around himself and cools down in his own fashion.

In summer, wash a sweaty horse down with a hose pipe, remove the surplus water with a scraper and then rub down with a wisp. In no time he will be dry and wonderfully clean.

Buying your own horse

ADVANTAGES
1 Unlimited riding at no extra cost
2 Freedom to ride when and where you will
3 Chances to take part in different horse activities
4 The *pleasure* of looking after and training it

DISADVANTAGES
1 6 gns per week at livery and not much less at home
2 Shoes every five weeks—£2 15s.
3 Saddle, girths, leathers, stainless steel stirrup irons, bridle, thick snaffle bit will cost from £50 to £75
4 Veterinary surgeon bills—2 gns. per visit at least
5 If the horse is incapacitated you are without a ride; a mount is always available at a school
6 If your horse is unsuitable, you may have difficulty in reselling it
7 If you look after him yourself, remember it is a daily task. No joke creeping out of bed and down to the stable with the flu. Your neighbour may look after your budgerigar but a horse is a different matter

Type of horse

All in all I suggest a free-moving cob type. Age about 7 years. Absolutely quiet in every way—traffic, shoeing. Well behaved in the stable. Easy to catch if you are turning out in the day-time or summer. Square, sound, not too big to climb aboard, not too far to fall off.

Appendix Two
Training the young horse

To ride well you need to understand the horse—you need to develop that feeling which tells you how a particular horse is going to behave. This can only be done with practise and by riding as many horses as possible.

In a brief, practical book like this there is no room to expand on this subject and, in any case, it is wearisome if the reader has not personal experience of many horses. But a potted picture of the horse as you now ride him can be given by considering the training of the young horse, for here it is not simply desirable, it is essential that the rider trainer understand him.

The job is not lightly undertaken and there is no room for learners, as you will see. Do not forget that the horse was not made to bear man—it is against all his instincts to tolerate something on his back. An enormous amount of time and work is needed to train him to the stage where he is strong and confident enough to carry a rider obediently.

Age

Too many horses are ridden too young. Thoroughbred horses, certainly, are raced at two years but these horses have been fed on oats almost before they were weaned and are then ridden by lightweight riders only.

It is not difficult to see why horses are ridden too young. A horse can be bought more cheaply at two or three years of age than at four; the public wants a cheap horse but also a trained horse; therefore the public gets a cheap, trained two-year-old. It is unfortunate for both parties. The horse is not strong enough either physically or mentally. Physically, his back will not support the rider's weight; he will suffer from a variety of leg troubles—splints and the like; he will, initially, always be changing his teeth—losing his milk teeth and getting his permanent set; with a bit in his mouth he cannot be expected to go kindly and an unsteady head will be his legacy.

His mental condition is not much better; 'Stress' is a word much in use today and it can seldom be more appropriately applied than to the ridden two- or three-year-old—by four he is either fed up, sour and 'nappy' or hot, temperamental and unreliable. There are no exceptions to this, though some animals take it better than others.

When to start, then? For a big horse, it is probably best to begin the training during the good weather of his third year. Lunging a strong, 16 hands thoroughbred out in the field on a cold, windy day is no joke. During this initial training session the horse can be taken to the point when he accepts a rider on his back; then he is roughed off and left to grow until he is about four; then the second session can start. During these periods the trainer must work the horse daily, on a progressive plan; he cannot go away on holiday, leaving the work to an assistant. Lessons are seldom more than an hour daily.

Why the horse is first trained on the lunge

Too many people think this is simply to make the horse obedient—moving round the trainer, walking, trotting and halting when commanded. Obedience is only a small part— an experienced trainer and responsive horse could achieve it in one day. The total is much more difficult: the trainer must reproduce, on the lunge and at his command, the true, natural paces that the horse possessed when moving in freedom. The fact that the horse has a cavesson head collar on him (extra weight) and is guided by the lunge line into a circle of the trainer's wish (not the horse's own) makes him lose his balance. He cannot throw his head about as a balancing pole; he cannot move in any direction; he must readjust to all this and find his natural movement.

1–3 days

He must be allowed to move on and track up; he must be persuaded to bend in the direction he is moving; he should give the same rounded appearance we look for over a jump; his head and neck must be exaggeratedly stretched down, in some cases until the nose is level with the knees.

After two days he is introduced to the bit. Each new lesson is always introduced at the end of a session and not before the previous one has been mastered or accepted.

4–7 days

Introduce the roller and side reins. The side reins must be very long and must allow the horse to stretch down into them. Seeking the bit. Looking towards the ground.

10–14 days

For the opening days the trainer himself walks in a small circle but now he starts to stand in one place rotating on his heel. This ensures that the horse is working in a true, round circle.

A whip is used in training: it must be long enough to reach the horse but it is rare that one needs do more than throw the thong towards the hocks to ask him to move forward, or towards the girth to keep him out to the end of the lunge or to make him bend correctly. By now the horse understands and responds to these whip aids and also to small vibrations down the lunge line, when a slowing down of rhythm is required.

During these days the roller is replaced by a stripped saddle.

Three weeks

Gradually the trainer asks for more impulsion: this makes the hocks, quarters and back muscles develop and lightens the forehand. Unless the back is made strong, with muscles developed by the rounding of the back and the seeking of the bit as he stretches down, he is going to dip in the middle when we put our weight on him—with consequent murdering of impulsion and stride.

Four weeks

The stirrup irons and leathers are put on to the saddle, so that he gets used to something touching his sides. The leathers must be short so that they do not bang against his elbows, for this hurts.

Introduction to a rider

It is about this time that a lightweight rider begins the lead up to mounting; it takes about a week of preliminaries before mounting is actually achieved.

Initially the rider leans against the saddle flap; then he is gradually legged up until he leans across the animal's back. It is often necessary to have a second assistant hold the horse on the right side; this prevents any swinging away of the quarters and misjudgement of the rider as he mounts.

When training any animal it is best to progress slowly and systematically. Things must not go wrong for this puts the horse back almost to the beginning.

At this stage, for example, if the rider misjudges the swing of the right leg over the back and gives the horse a hefty kick on the quarters, he will have the fright of his life, buck, break loose, buck the half-seated rider off and gallop off in panic. A good trainer will undoubtedly overcome this setback but the memory of the fright will never leave the horse. At some future date, when the horse is fresh and perhaps cold, a touch on the quarters while mounting will carry him back to his four-year-old days and off he will go. Horses learn by association of ideas and woe betide if the association is unpleasant!

Five weeks

During the week, mounting is generally achieved; the horse is at first led forward one step, then two and finally lunged with the rider on. The trainer directs the rider to control the horse, firstly by use of the voice and then a combination of voice and leg and then voice and rein. Finally, by association of ideas, he responds to the leg alone.

Six weeks

The horse is now off the lunge, working in a small paddock. Another, trained horse may be introduced as a school master. It is important that the school master is not used to give a lead to the young horse continually but that the young horse learns to pass and repass the older animal, to move both toward and away from it. Things cannot be rushed—the horse must both step forward freely and with impulsion and must also be obedient and quiet, gaining confidence in the rider. The trainer, has, in fact, to be extremely knowledgeable, to make sure, at this stage, that the horse's natural stride is preserved. It is so easy to flatten out the horse, get the head and neck too high, chop and ruin the stride for all time.

Winter break

If the horse needs more time to grow and develop, this is the time to end this session of training, rest him through the winter and start again in March or April. If the training is so stopped, three weeks retraining is required to reach the stage where we left him previously.

4–6 weeks, second session

He is worked along straight lines with a light long rein, gradually introduced to up and downhill slopes, large circles on the easy rein (i.e. which way he likes to bend) and then the more difficult rein.

6–8 weeks, second session

He has already been lunged over poles on the ground and now, with the rider aboard, he steps and then trots over them. In due course he pops over tree trunks, etc. He must be allowed to jump with a loose rein for he has to learn to get himself out of muddles now, while the fences are so low. When he is used to stepping through shallow flood water he can be asked to jump into it; care is needed, for a horse doesn't like jumping into water.

The horse is introduced to a variety of ground surfaces— gravel paths, turf, plough, heavy mud (the first time it kicks up under his belly can be a nasty moment), sand.

He has to adapt to traffic. No doubt he has already seen vehicles arriving at the yard; he should be mounted and standing nearby when cars come and go; he must obviously not be forced up to them. He is taken out along suitable roads in the company of one or two school masters; their presence will help him to remain calm. Avoid the unusual, e.g. lorries with flapping covers.

The horse is broadening his outlook, learning to work and concentrate wherever he is, gaining confidence through the greater control of the rider. His jumping is progressing and he now approaches small fences at a trot, so that he can best judge the position for take off. Eventually, as the canter becomes more balanced and less on the forehand, he jumps from a canter. He must not be allowed to frighten himself by meeting fences wrong, especially as the jumps get bigger.

Three months, second session

By now the horse is working in different areas, sometimes on his own, sometimes with another quiet horse; he leaves his school master at one end of the paddock and works with a fair measure of concentration in the centre of the field: large circles, both left and right, in all paces, moving straight; over 2 ft. 6 in. fences, generally from the trot; when trotting he learns to lengthen the stride and slow down the rhythm.

Jumping and work up and down hill, bending left and right, have strengthened the hocks and back; he can now be asked for more impulsion without a speeding of rhythm. Changing from trot to walk and walk to trot, then up to canter and down again also develop this. Most horses find these transitions difficult and the rider may go back to using more voice when slowing down. It would be disastrous to use more rein.

Throughout all this training, the rider has been riding shorter than when riding an older, trained horse, and sitting light, using little, if any seat. This is because the young horse must be encouraged to bring his back up under the saddle. Now, after three months, he can begin to sit deeper.

Now also, the horse progresses to more specialised work. The crucial months are over.

Consider, then, the horse

When a novice first goes to a riding school, the horse must seem a 'given' factor, an animal who simply behaves according to a pattern, provided that he, the rider, does the right thing.

The above programme demonstrates better than anything that this is not the case. Think of the immense skill required by the trainer in judging just what he must do; the horse does not naturally do any of these things and yet, when the novice rides him for the first time, he obeys, provided he understands what his rider wants.

So then, at all times consider the horse, try to understand him. From first to last, that is the way to good riding.